Silk Ribbons
by Machine

Silk Ribbons *by* Machine

Jeanie Sexton

American Quilter's Society

P. O. Box 3290 • Paducah, KY 42002-3290

Located in Paducah, Kentucky, the American Quilter's Society (AQS), is dedicated to promoting the accomplishments of today's quilters. Through its publications and events, AQS strives to honor today's quiltmakers and their work – and inspire future creativity and innovation in quiltmaking.

Library of Congress Cataloging-in-Publication Data

Sexton, Jeanie.
    Silk ribbons by machine / Jeanie Sexton.
        p. cm.
    Includes bibliographical references.
    ISBN 0-89145-880-8
        1. Silk ribbon embroidery.   2. Embroidery, Machine – Patterns.
    I. Title.
    TT778.S64S48   1996
    746.44–dc20   96-9202
                                                                        CIP

Additional copies of this book may be ordered from: American Quilter's Society,
P.O. Box 3290, Paducah, KY 42002-3290 @ $15.95. Add $2.00 for postage & handling.

Printed in the U.S.A. by Image Graphics

Dedication

This book is dedicated to the loving memory of my mother and grandmother who made me learn to sew when I would rather have been climbing an apple tree. They always reminded me that all talent is a gift from God to cultivate and share.

A Special Thank You

To Meredith Schroeder and Bonnie Browning for encouraging me to write this book. To Charley Lynch for his expertise in photographing my samples, to Marcie Hinton for editing, and Elaine Wilson for her computer expertise.

To Linda and Keith English for sponsoring my classes and encouraging me to expand beyond Paducah.

To Sharee Dawn Roberts for introducing me to machine arts and the world of embellishment.

To my sisters, Jane and Jody, who encourage my inspirations, even at midnight when I have an idea to run by them.

To Herb who supports me in all my creative endeavors and loves me enough to allow space for my sewing machine and computer in our lives.

To my son, Duke, for sharing his knowledge of the computer and camera.

To my students and friends, especially Marilyn and Rachel, who challenge me to come up with new techniques to share.

Contents

Introduction

Believe it or not you can stitch those beautiful silk ribbon flowers with your sewing machine. This book presents an unconventional method to achieve this traditional skill. I can't wait to share it with fellow ardent machine artists. The machine stitches will not show – that is my secret to your success!

Several basic stitches will be illustrated that can be used for many different flowers by simply changing silk ribbon colors and widths. Color photographs will inspire you to copy my work at first, then try it on your own. Detailed illustrations and chronological steps guide you through each sample.

We will begin with single flowers, then simple arrangements on sketched line drawings. When you feel comfortable, you can move on to the more complicated designs, such as the woven flower basket. Before long you will be sketching your own flower gardens and taking time to smell the roses!

I have always admired handwork but just do not have the patience to relax and complete many projects. My crochet stitching is so tight I need help to pull it off my fingers. Needless to say, machine techniques are very relaxing to me, so finding a way to machine stitch the gorgeous silk ribbon flowers was a must! Of course, the idea of completing a project in an hour or so appeals to me too.

After studying illustrations for hand stitching, I simplified and adapted the designs to my sewing machine. It took practice to learn to relax and allow the ribbons to flow softly and naturally. Silk ribbon has a personality of its own, much like the flowers we are trying to duplicate.

Thank you for allowing me to share this unique technique with you.

May All Your Ribbons Be Romantic,
Jeanie Sexton

Inspiration for Ideas

Since starting to experiment with silk ribbon embroidery by machine, I seem to view flowers in a different manner. When I see flower motifs, I now envision ways to duplicate them by using basic ribbon embroidery stitches.

Being a country girl, I have enjoyed flowers all my life. I have fond memories of my grandparents' farm with wild flowers in the woods and Mammy's yard full of special flowers. When searching for an idea, I usually think of her hollyhocks, gladiolus, zinnias, tulips, and tea roses.

Use flower seed catalogs for color choices. It is a fun and challenging way to create the petals and clusters of flowers. Look at the illustrations in these catalogs as well. The ways the flowers are arranged into gardens and settings offer excellent ideas for placement of the silk ribbon flowers.

I have also found inspiration in magazine ads for perfumes and cosmetics that use bouquets. These are great because the arrangements are completed. All you have to do is substitute your ribbon flowers.

Real silk flower arrangements, wallpaper borders and home decor, wrapping paper, lingerie, and greeting cards all use floral arrangements in their designs, so you definitely don't have to be an artist to create embroidery patterns. I have even been inspired by the tulip bouquets on my shower curtain!

Machine artists love to share inspiration and ideas with each other, so blend your friends' machine embroidery patterns with your silk ribbon embroidery motifs.

Silk Ribbons by Machine

Ribbons

Each silk ribbon design can be completed using the same basic stitches. The magic appears when you change the ribbon colors and widths to create so many different flowers and leaves.

In selecting your color palette, try to include both warm and cool colors. The warm colors are the yellows, golds, reds, and browns. The cool colors are the blues, greens, and purples. White can be a cool or warm color; the cool tone is a rather stark white, while the warm tone is a softer antique white. You will need a mixture of greens which are dyed in both warm and cool hues. There are some beautiful hand-dyed ribbons which flow from shade to shade. These stitch into very realistic floral colors. After the flower shades are selected, your eye will determine whether to select the warm or cool complementary green shades.

Illustrations of interchangeable colors using the basic daisy flower straight stitches include: white petals with yellow centers for daisies; gold petals with brown centers for sunflowers; or gold petals with black centers for black-eyed Susans. See how easy it is!

We will use three sizes of ribbons: 2mm (¹⁄₁₆"), 4mm (⅛"), and 7mm (¼"). The ribbon widths are as interchangeable as the colors. For example, use 7mm for the large flowers and leaves, 4mm for medium sizes, and 2mm for the tiny ones. The 2mm size creates the most delicate French knots, while the 7mm creates the largest softest roses and lazy daisy stitches.

Any brand of ribbon can be used. You will need to press the creases out of the carded ribbons though. Be careful and test the iron setting on the tip of the silk ribbon. A unique way of pressing out soft folds is to run the ribbon across the metal shade of your sewing lamp because it can get so hot.

Test ribbons for colorfastness by dipping the end in water. If it bleeds on a white paper towel, wash the ribbon.

Fabrics

This is where the machine embroidered silk ribbon technique is more versatile than hand stitching. You can use even the tightest woven fabrics because the ribbons don't have to be pulled through the fabric. For beginners, a tightly woven fabric is suggested. After becoming comfortable with the stitches, go on to the knits. The difference is the loosely woven fabrics will need to be stabilized with lightweight fusible interfacing before hooping.

Choose any fabrics from cottons and satins to velvets and tapestries for your background fabrics. A spring hoop is suggested for embroidering on velvets to keep from crushing the nap. After unhooping, lay face down on a towel and steam press (only the crushed fabric, not the ribbon area). Turn over and hold the iron above the fabric and allow the steam to "puff up" the nap a little more. If you have to leave your project for any length of time, remove velvet from the hoop. This will prevent a deep crease in the velvet nap.

Supplies

The primary piece of equipment you will need for silk ribbon embroidery is your sewing machine. Your machine needs to be clean, oiled, and in good working condition. The feed dogs must have the capability of being lowered or covered with a plate. Also, you will want to completely remove the ankle and/or the foot.

Experiment and adjust your machine settings for your individual make and model. If your normal sewing tension is 5, and you use a tension of +3- for automatic machine embroidery and 1 – 2 tension for free-motion embroidery, select a tension of +2- for silk ribbon embroidery. If your bobbin thread is pulled to the top, lower the needle tension until it

Silk Ribbons by Machine

disappears. Needle down function should be engaged if your machine has this feature.

Besides the machine, a built in cabinet or an extension table for your machine is a worthwhile investment. Most sewing machine companies have portable tables available to fit your make and model. The table has more surface for the embroidery hoop to rest upon. It won't fall off the edge of the sewing machine.

You will also need a new #70/10 needle. You should have several needles on hand because if you have a burr on the needle, it will snag the fine ribbons. A #70/10 Microtex® needle, which has a very sharp eye for machine embroidery, works wonderfully on natural fibers such as cotton doilies. The eye just barely pokes a hole. The smaller hole prevents the bobbin thread from being pulled to the surface.

While on the subject of needles, you will need a chenille needle to pull the ends of the ribbons to the back. This is a hand needle with a large eye and sharp point. The eye end of the needle can be used to fluff up the ribbons when you are finished.

We will use a very fine (.004) clear monofilament thread in the needle. This is the trick to the special effects giving machine embroidery the appearance of hand embroidery. We do not stitch on the ribbons but jump over and gather them; therefore, the needle thread never shows.

Because we are sewing with invisible thread, your supplies may need to include a tiny halogen light shining beside the needle which adds just enough extra lighting to the workspace. Also a pair of inexpensive reading glasses keeps the eyestrain down to a minimum.

The bobbin thread needs to be a white 50-wt. cotton thread. You may use whichever bobbin thread you use with free-motion embroidery. When embroidering on a dark or ready-made fabric that is unlined, use the same color in the bobbin. This gives a more finished appearance on the wrong side. Also, if the bobbin thread comes to the top from time to time, it will blend with the fabric.

I recommend using a wooden machine embroidery hoop with the inner ring wrapped with one layer of muslin strips. A spring hoop will work, but the wooden hoop will hold the fabric tighter.

Sharp embroidery scissors will be needed to allow you to get in close to the fabric when clipping threads and ribbons. The scissors should not have a burr on them because this will snag the fine ribbons.

Long tweezers will be used to hold the ribbons. Select tweezers which are comfortable in your hand. The ones that came with my serger are long and skinny with a curved tip and work well with this technique.

A water or air soluble pen is necessary to mark the pattern on your fabric. If you are going to stitch immediately, you can use an air soluble pen. If using a water soluble pen, pretest the fabric first to make sure the marker rinses away.

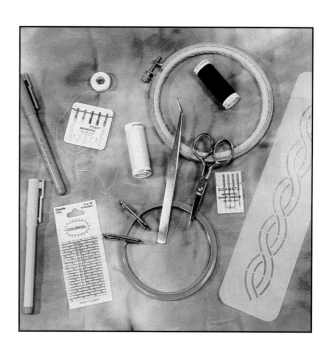

Plate 1.

Supplies used for machine silk ribbons.

General Instructions

Instead of putting your nose in front of the needle as with normal machine embroidery, sit just left of the needle (toward the end of the machine). This way you can see all around the needle, not just in front of it. Until you become relaxed with this new technique you may find that you have lower back strain. To avoid lower back aches, use the best chair you can afford. If your chair has a height adjustment, try lowering it a little. Your backache should ease as you relax and flow with the ribbons. And, as always, use good posture!

In order to simplify the visual aide, the same color codes will be carried throughout the stitch symbols, stitch instructions, projects, and illustrated patterns.

The narrative with the photographs of chronological steps is condensed. Please follow the detailed directions when practicing the stitches. In order for the machine stitches to show in the photographs, dark threads are used in the needle. Ribbons are sometimes pulled to the side to show the machine stitches. Always manipulate the ribbons to cover the monofilament thread.

MARKING MOTIF

The entire design doesn't have to be traced on background fabric. Dots and dashes are sufficient.

Trace the outline on transparent paper. Deli paper is a very inexpensive tracing paper. (It is a wax-free translucent sandwich wrap which can be purchased at most janitorial supply stores.) Onion skin typing paper works equally well.

After tracing the outline, make holes along the drawn lines about ⅛" to ¼" apart with a thick pointed crewel needle.

Position the dotted pattern where you want it on the background fabric and secure it in the corners with pins.

With an air or water soluble pen, make dots on the fabric through the holes. Unpin the paper, connect the dots on the vine lines, and you are ready to embroider your beautiful ribbon flowers.

Figure 1.

Figure 2.

You can also trace the standard way using a light box or window. The hole punched technique is great for dark colors. Use a white chalk pencil for the dots.

A small quilting template can also be used to sketch in vine lines on lapels. These have some pretty curved patterns. Randomly add leaves and flowers wherever you want them.

Stencils for sponge painting come in tiny floral motifs and can also be used as templates.

Another useful tool is a template which has different sized circle holes. When beginning to embroider, you may want to use the different sized holes for your markings. Although silk ribbon flowers are free formed, the markings help to make them relatively the same size. With a water or air soluble pen, draw the sizes you want using the template. As a guide for the petals, make lines across the circle, ending at the edges (Fig. 1).

A simple way to draw a fern frond is to sketch a fat curved leaf with a vein in the center. Make lines on each side of the vein to the edge of the leaf. Add one line at the tip, then erase the outer lines. It will look like a skeleton of a leaf (Fig. 2).

HOOPING FABRIC

It is best to have a variety of sizes of hoops on hand. You will want the hoop to encircle the entire area you are working on, so you won't crush the previously embroidered flowers. Sometimes you may only have enough room between flowers to embroider one at a time. This is where a tiny 3" hoop comes in handy. This size is great for collars and cuffs also. If you must crush an embroidered area, try to place the hoop on a vine.

Use a wooden machine embroidery hoop. It is narrower and is designed for use with the sewing machine. Wrap the inner ring with strips of muslin or bias tape (Plate 2). This keeps the fabric from slipping. The fabric does not need to be stretched drum tight as with machine embroidery, it just needs to be taut. You will be stitching just opposite of hand embroidery, where the outer ring with fabric is facing up. The outer ring and fabric will be against the throat plate. You will be embroidering

inside the bowl.

Place the outer ring on the table, fabric right side up, then inner (wrapped) ring within them. Tighten the screw with your fingers. Stretch the fabric with the grain in all directions. Tighten the screw with a screwdriver. This allows the hoop to hold the fabric tighter. Now pull the fabric again with the grain. Press the inner ring about ⅛" to the back to give more tension and allow the ring to move easier on the machine.

One advantage of using a spring embroidery hoop is it can be moved more quickly from area to area. Prepare the ring and fabric the same way as with the wooden machine embroidery hoop. Slightly stretch the fabric with the grain. Re-stretch if fabric becomes slack. If there are wrinkles after removing the hoop, they can be steam pressed out.

If the area you are embroidering is not large enough to hoop the edges, baste a piece of muslin a couple of inches larger than the hoop to the back of the fabric, centering the area to be embroidered. Turn over and carefully cut away the center area (where you will embroider), leaving a frame of muslin to be hooped. Hoop as usual. (See page 16.) When the stitching is complete, remove from the

Plate 2.
Wooden embroidery hoop, wrapped with muslin.

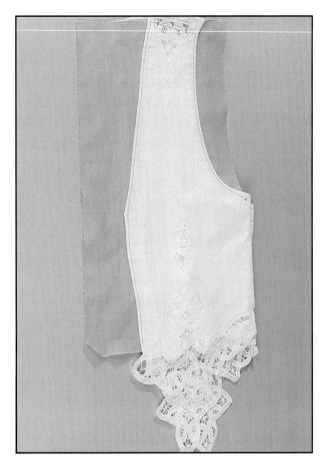

Plate 3, top left.
Back of vest, fabric cut away leaving embroidery area.

Plate 4, top right.
Front of vest with fabric around the edges.

Plate 5, left.
Front of vest, hooped area was too small before adding the fabric on the edges.

hoop, remove basted muslin, and press as usual. Wide satin and grosgrain ribbons for hats and trims can be machine embroidered with the silk ribbons using this same method. Embellish hats, purses, clothes, etc. by straight stitching along the outer edges with matching rayon thread.

FINISHING

Remove the finished piece from the hoop. Snip any untidy threads from the back. Mend the needle holes with your fingernail or the tweezer's edge by rubbing against the grain, pushing the threads into the original weave. With a damp sponge, remove any markings which may still show. Steam press, face up, around the edges of the embroidered ribbon motifs. Be careful not to touch the silk ribbons. Press up and down so the fabric won't stretch.

If there are ribbon ends or threads laying beyond the embroidered areas, glue them away from the edge (back on the stitching where they belong) with a tiny dot of "stop fraying" glue. The ribbon ends may show through to the right side of light colored fabric.

Now, take the eye end of your chenille needle or the tip of your tweezers and fluff up the petals a little bit. Hold the steam iron about 1" above the flowers and allow the steam to flow on the flowers. Give them a burst of steam if your iron has this capability and watch them come to life! While they are damp, manipulate the petals.

Stitches

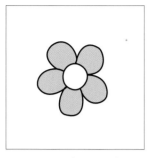

Straight Stitch

*Straight Stitch Leaves &
Stem Stitch Vines*

Chain Stitch

Chain Stitch Center

Curl and Flip Stitch

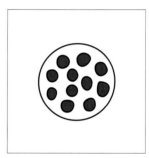

French Knot Center

Bullion Stitches

Curved Bullion Center

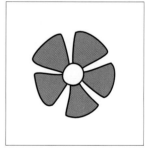

Stacked Straight Stitch

Looped Straight Stitch

*Layered Looped
Straight Stitch*

Fern Frond

Silk Ribbons by Machine

Basic Jump Stitch

Jump stitching is accomplished using the conventional machine set-up for free-motion embroidery. Remember to lower the presser bar to allow the stitches to form and to avoid a bird's nest on the back. Also, you will have formed a flower which will pull out very easily. Most sewing machines have a darning or free-motion embroidery position for the presser bar. Check your manual for the adjustment

Now for the embroidery. Each stitch is formed exactly the same way. All you do is jump over the ribbons.

Place hooped fabric under the needle. Lower the presser bar and draw up the bobbin thread. Take a few stitches in place to secure the threads. Stitch a short distance away and clip the thread ends. Secure the end of the ribbon a couple of inches from the end by stitching across it a couple of times. Cut off the end. This will usually be covered up with more ribbons. If there is a stitch which needs this end to be pulled to the back, it will be addressed in the individual stitch section. When you have finished a color of ribbon, cut the ribbon on an angle leaving a 3" tail. Thread into the chenille needle and pull to the back. Tie three times with the bobbin thread and cut, leaving about ½" tail. When tying the ends together, manipulate the bobbin thread rather than the ribbon to avoid a big knot. Loop the thread around the ribbon and slide it to the base of the ribbon. Pull on the thread to tighten the slip knot. Repeat twice.

Place the needle in the down position. Hold the ribbon against the needle (on its side) with the tweezers in one hand and between your finger and thumb of the other hand. Tap the foot pedal once and take one stitch in place to secure the stitch. Now take one stitch over the top of the ribbon to the other side. Take an additional stitch in place to secure the stitch. This will allow the ribbon to gather. Try not to stitch into the ribbons, but over them. Also try not to pierce the ribbon and split it. If it happens though, just fluff the ribbon around the stitch when you finish the petal or leaf. Now simply manipulate the hoop, tweezers, and ribbons as instructed in the individual stitching sections. The reason for securing individual stitches is to lock the needle thread with the bobbin thread. If you move the hoop too quickly, before the stitch is completed, the bobbin thread will come to the top. This will also happen if the fabric is not held down against the throat plate. With practice you will learn to relax.

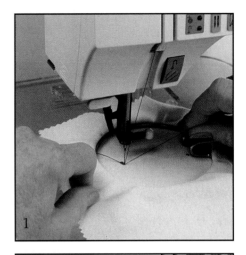

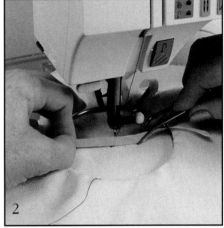

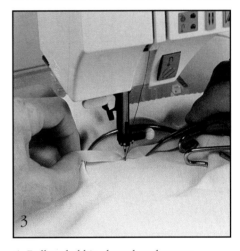

1. *Pull up bobbin thread and secure.*
2. *Hold ribbon against needle.*
3. *Jump stitch to front, gathering ribbon, secure stitch.*

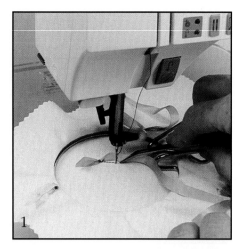

Straight Stitch

The basic straight stitch will be used for most of the leaves.

- Secure ribbon.
- Stitch a traveling line about ½" in the direction you want to position your leaf. (#1)
- Gently hold the ribbon against the needle and jump over it, gathering it. This is the tip. (#2)
- Take an additional stitch in place to secure the stitch. Try to avoid stitching into the ribbon.
- Hold the end of the ribbon to the side and stitch a traveling line beside the secured ribbon to its base. (#3)
- Gently hold the ribbon against the needle and jump over it, gathering it. The ribbon should lay softly against the first one or slightly overlap it. (#4)
- Take an additional stitch in place to secure the stitch.
- Cut ribbons on an angle, thread into chenille needle, pull to back and tie with bobbin threads. Now you have completed one straight stitch.

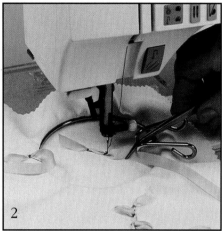

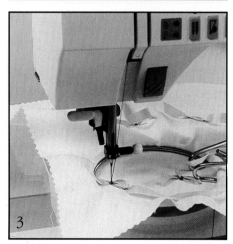

1. Jump stitch to secure ribbon, travel to tip.
2. Jump stitch.
3. Travel to base.
4. Hold ribbon against needle, jump stitch gathering ribbon, secure stitch.

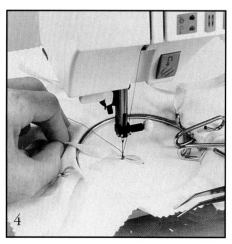

Stem Stitch

For the stem stitch, the ribbon will be stitched in a way that resembles a hand straight stitch. The stitches should be the length of a hand stitched straight stitch (about ½"). You can also make it about ¼" to create a stem to attach a leaf or bud to the edge of a vine.

- Secure ribbon. (#1)
- Stitch about ½". (#2)
- Twist ribbon a few times.
- Jump stitch over to secure and take an additional stitch in place to secure the stitch.
- Continue by twisting, and jump stitching, securing the last stitch by stitching into the ribbon. (#3)
- Cut ribbon ends on angle, thread into chenille needle, pull both ends to back and tie with bobbin threads.

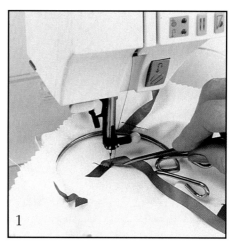

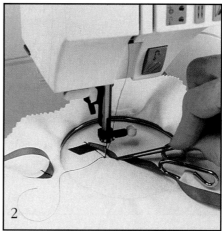

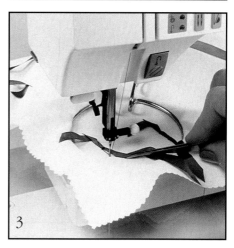

1. Secure ribbon, twist ribbon.
2. Travel.
3. Jump stitch, completed stem stitched vine.

Stacked Straight Stitch

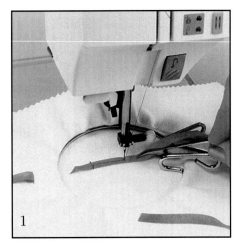

The stacked straight stitch makes a beautiful fern frond which is excellent to fill in open areas or beneath flowers.

This stitch also creates a flat daisy flower. The directions are the same as for the straight stitch without gathering the ends.

- Secure ribbon. This will be the base of the leaf or petal.
- Lay the ribbon flat and stitch up the center to the tip. Stitch on the ribbon. (#1)
- Stitch across the end of the ribbon. Stitch on the ribbon. This is the tip of the leaf or petal.
- Hold the end of ribbon up and travel back down the center of the secured ribbon to its base. (#2)
- Fold the loose end of the ribbon over the top of the previously secured ribbon. (#3)
- At the base of the leaf or petal stitch across the ribbon to secure the top ribbon. Secure the stitch. (#4)
- Cut ribbons on an angle, thread into chenille needle, pull to back and tie with bobbin threads. Now you have completed one stacked straight stitch. (#5)

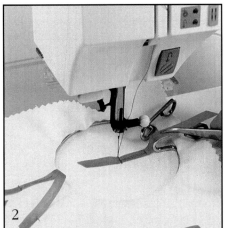

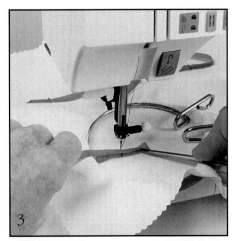

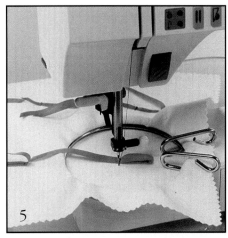

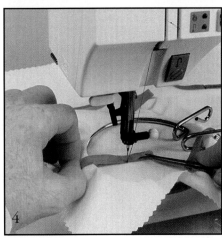

1. Secure ribbon, travel on ribbon to tip.
2. Travel across tip and back to base.
3. Fold ribbon over against needle.
4. Secure at base.
5. Completed stacked straight stitch.

Looped Straight Stitch

The looped straight stitch is actually half of the procedure for the straight stitch. You simply do not secure the outer loops, leaving them soft and fluffy.

- Secure ribbon. Clip off end.
- Lay the edge of the ribbon along where you want the petal to be positioned.
- Make a loop at the end of the petal and hold it gently with the tweezers.
- Bring the loose end of the ribbon back to the base of the petal, in front of the needle. (#1)
- Gently hold the ribbon against the needle and jump over it, gathering it. (#2)
- Take an additional stitch into the ribbon to secure it at the base.
- Continue around the inner circle, jumping in front of the ribbons, until the flower is completed. (#3)
- Cut ribbon on an angle, thread into chenille needle, pull to back and tie with bobbin thread.

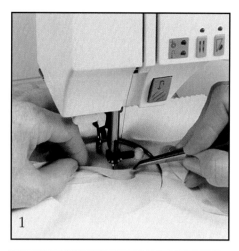

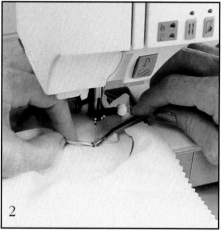

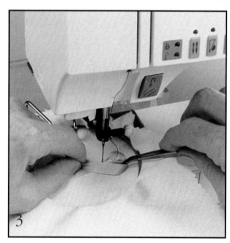

1. Jump stitch to secure ribbon, pull ribbon in front of needle.
2. Jump stitch to front of ribbon.
3. Pull new loop to front of needle.

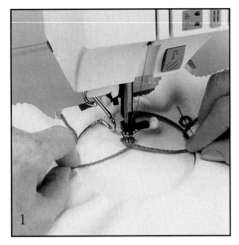

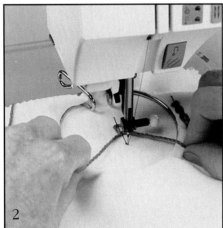

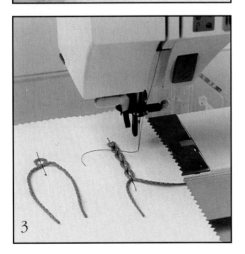

1. Secure cord, cross ends.
2. Jump over intersection and travel.
3. Completed chain.

Chain Stitch

The chain stitch is a beautiful addition to machine stitched silk ribbon motifs. A row of chain stitches can stand alone as vines or be used to connect and separate motifs. Tiny cords can be stitched as stamens and centers of flowers. A row of chain stitches can outline a basket motif, then fill in the center area. Rows can be stitched in a grid to portray a trellis which can be covered with tiny flowers.

All size cords and silk ribbons can be used for the chain stitch. The silk ribbons can be left flat and gathered or twisted as instructed with the stem stitch. Begin with a length of cord or silk ribbon twice the length you desire to stitch plus 6". With a little practice, you can determine the necessary lengths according to the closeness of the stitches. Begin with more than you think you will need.

- Find the center of the cord. Jump stitch to secure it where you plan to begin stitching.
- Stitch about three stitches in front of the cords.
- Pull the cords to the front of the needle, cross over each other and hold to each side with fingertips about 1" away from the needle. (#1)
- Jump stitch across the crossed cords.
- Make an additional stitch or two to secure the stitch. Then make three more traveling stitches. (#2)
- Cross the cords in front of the needle and repeat the process until desired distance is stitched. (#3)
- Stitch across cords to secure, cut, pull to the back with the chenille needle, and tie with bobbin thread.

Curl and Flip Stitch

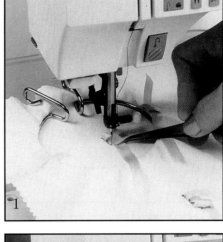

The curl and flip stitch can be used when you need a corkscrew effect for a flower or a coiled stream of ribbon to accent your motif. You can make them in rows using as many flips as needed or in a circle leaving the center open for French knots. This is beautiful for statice on a stem. After you master the stitch, you can create the dainty tea roses.

- Secure the ribbon, leaving a 3" tail on the right side of the needle.

- With the tweezers, curl and hold the ribbon flat against the throat plate so it extends to the left of the needle. (#1)

- Stitch toward yourself about half way across the ribbon then back off the ribbon where stitching began. (#2)

- Hold the ribbon up and slightly angle it toward yourself. (#3)

- Stitch under the ribbon, then travel an additional ribbon width.

- Allow the ribbon to curl over itself to the right and toward the needle. Softly flip it and hold flat against the throat plate with the tweezers (corkscrew effect).

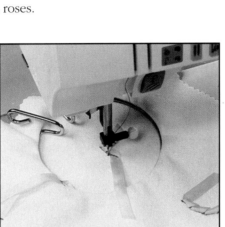

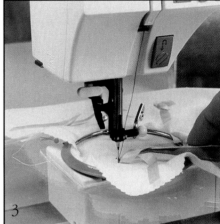

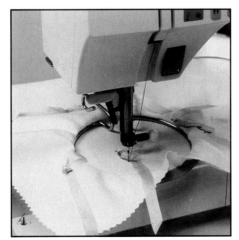

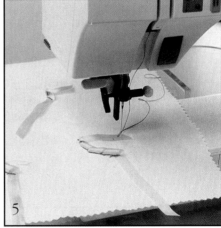

- Stitch toward yourself about half way across the ribbon then back off the ribbon where stitching began, as with the first curl. Repeat until you have a sufficient number of corkscrews. (#4)

- To finish, stitch across the ribbon and back as though making a curl, cut ribbon leaving a 3" tail.

- Using the chenille needle, flip the ribbon as though making another curl. Pull to the back leaving a soft roll on the top. Tie both ribbon ends with bobbin threads.

1. Secure ribbon, travel under needle. Flip ribbon to right and lay flat.
2. Stitch on and off ribbon.
3. Curl ribbon.
4. Travel under ribbon. Stitch on and off.
5. Curl ribbon over to cover stitches.

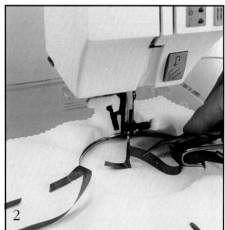

Bullion Stitch

The bullion stitch can be used alone or as a filler, much like the French knot. The only difference is ribbon is always used instead of cords. They can be laid straight for use as buds or side by side for flowers, using straight stitch leaves around them.

- Secure the ribbon by stitching across the end. Clip off the tail. You will cover up this end.
- Hold the ribbon up flat against the needle. (#1)
- Rotate the hoop 3 to 6 times, gently wrapping the ribbon around the needle. (#2)
- Hold the wraps with the first finger and thumb of your left hand. Take your foot off the pedal. (#3)
- Allow the ribbon wrap to loosen just enough to slip off the needle. (If they are real tight the needle thread will break.) Hold the loops and fabric against the throat plate.
- With your left fingers still gently holding the ribbon wrap, turn the fly wheel toward yourself with your right hand, slipping the ribbon wrap off the needle. Lay the ribbon down straight across the clipped end. (#4)
- Lay the ribbon wrap so the end appears to reel off the bottom, not across the top; flat on the fabric rather than covering up your pretty coil of ribbon.
- Stitch across the flat loose end to secure the ribbon wrap. (#5)
- Clip ribbon end on an angle, thread into chenille needle, pull to the back and tie with bobbin thread.
- Gently roll the ribbon coil over to hide the first clipped end. (#6)

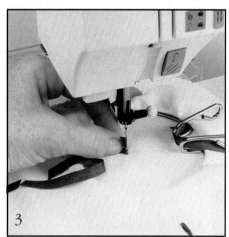

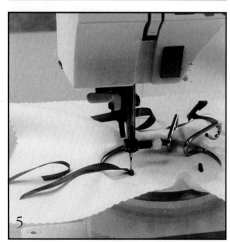

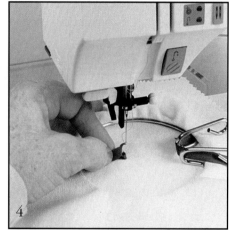

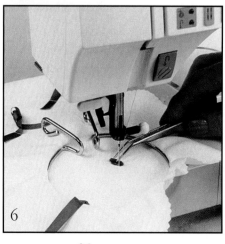

Curved Bullion Stitch

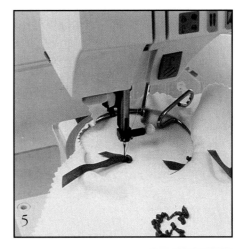

The curved bullion stitch is the same as the bullion stitch except it is laid in curves and coils to make clusters of wisteria and Queen Anne's lace. The width of the ribbon determines the resulting flower.

- Secure the ribbon by stitching across the end. Clip off the tail. This end will be covered up.
- Hold the ribbon flat against the needle. (#1, page 26)
- Rotate the hoop 3 to 6 times, gently wrapping the ribbon around the needle. (#2, page 26)
- Hold the wraps with the first finger and thumb of your left hand. Take your foot off the pedal. (#3, page 26)
- Allow the ribbon wrap to loosen just enough to slip off the needle. (If they are really tight the needle thread will break.) Hold the loops and fabric against the throat plate.
- With your left fingers still gently holding the ribbon wrap, turn the fly wheel toward yourself with your right hand, slipping the ribbon wrap off the needle. (#4, page 26) This time allow the ribbon wrap to gently curve as you position it. (#5)
- Do not put stress on the needle because it will bend and break if it hits the throat plate.
- Using the fly wheel, place the needle into the fabric. Take a few stitches to secure the ribbon wrap.
- For a cluster of coils and curves, after completing one stitch, secure the ribbon end, travel by loosely twisting it and jump stitching over it to where you want to position the next coil or curve. (#6)
- Secure each ribbon and continue to make ribbon wraps.
- When the area is filled in to your satisfaction, secure the last ribbon wrap by stitching across the end. (#7)
- Clip ribbon end on an angle, thread into chenille needle, pull to the back and tie with bobbin thread. Gently roll the ribbon coil over to hide the clipped end.

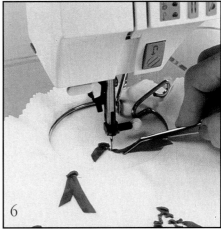

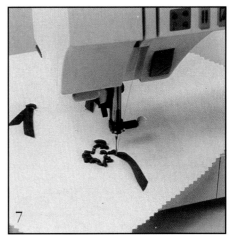

See steps 1 – 4 of bullion stitch, page 26.
5. Curve ribbon, lay down, secure end.
6. Twist and jump stitch to travel.
7. Cluster of stitches.

Opposite page
1. Secure ribbon, hold ribbon up.
2. Wrap around needle.
3. Hold wrap.
4. Loosen wrap and bring needle out.
5. Lay down ribbon, stitch across end.
6. Secure ribbon and clip end, roll ribbon over.

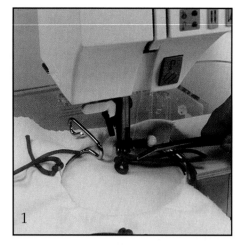

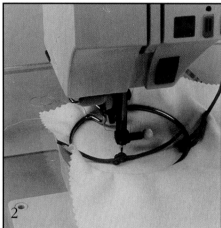

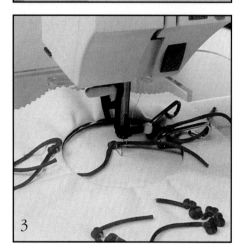

1. Tie double knot around needle.
2. Jump stitch to outside to secure knot.
3. Travel.

French Knots

French knots can stand alone as clusters of tiny baby's breath and to fill in a sparse area. They are used most frequently as flower centers and pistils. Experiment with different ply cords, yarns, and ribbon widths. The area to be filled in will determine how many wraps you will need. An 8" to 10" length is plenty to use for each cluster of knots.

- Place the needle down in the fabric. Tie a soft double knot around the needle at the center of the cord. (#1)
- Place the ends of the cord to each side of the needle and hold them down to the throat plate with your fingertips about 1" away from the needle.
- Make a stitch outside the knot. (#2)
- Make another stitch to secure the stitch.
- Travel about 1/16" and leave the needle down in the fabric. (#3)
- Bring one of the ends to the needle. Rotate the hoop 3 to 6 times, wrapping the cord around the needle.
- Hold the loops with your left first finger and thumb. Take your foot off the pedal. (#4)
- Allow the loops to loosen just enough to slip off the needle. (If they are real tight the needle thread will break.) Hold the loops and fabric against the throat plate.
- With your left fingers still on the knot and the needle down in the fabric, turn the fly wheel toward yourself with your right hand, slipping the knot off the needle.
- Make a stitch in place, take another back into the knot and out again.
- Gently tug on the end of the cord. tightening the knot a little. If it is still too loose and floppy, just stitch over the cord to secure it. You may jump stitch back into and out of the knot.
- Travel and continue making additional knots until the area is filled in. Use the other end of the cord when you get to that area; or just pull it to the back when the French knots are completed. (#5)
- Pull ends of the cords to the back and tie each end with the bobbin thread.
- Use your fingernails to scrunch up the knots by squeezing all around the edges. This will make the center higher and more dense.

Silk Ribbons by Machine

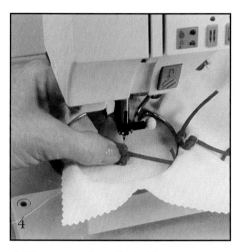 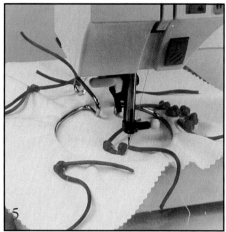

4. Wrap around needle, hold wrap.
5. Lay cord over and secure, travel and stitch more knots.

Motifs

PUTTING BASIC STITCHES TOGETHER TO CREATE A MOTIF

The key to putting together the basic stitches is to relax and loosen up. More than likely, your first embroideries will be tight. The more you get used to the flow, the looser it will get. After creating a few designs, the embroidery will look more like it was hand stitched.

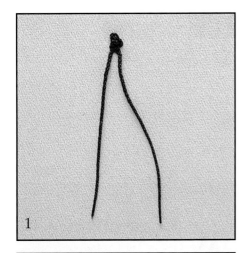

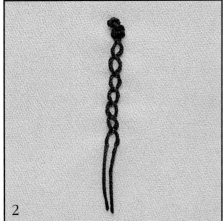

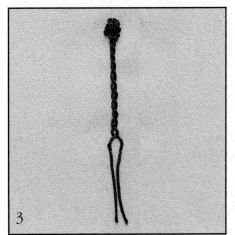

Pistils and Stamens

The French knot and the chain stitch are used to make the tiny pistils and stamens of flowers. Just begin at the tip of the stamen and make a French knot in the center of the cord. After securing it, pull the cords around to the front of the needle and secure. Make a row of chain stitches to just beyond the edge of where the tip of the petal will appear. Pull the cords to the back and tie with the bobbin thread. Stitch the petals so the tips cover the stamen's beginning.

1. French knot.
2. French knot and chain stitches.
3. Completed motif.

Silk Ribbons by Machine

Leaves

Leaves are a combination of the stem stitch and the straight stitch.

- Secure ribbon.
- Stitch about ¼". (This is the stem or beginning of the vine.)
- Twist ribbon a few times.
- Couch over to secure and make an additional stitch in place to secure the stitch.
- Stitch a traveling line about ½" in the direction you want to position the leaf.
- Gently hold the ribbon against the needle and jump over it, gathering it. This is the tip.
- Make an additional stitch in place to secure the stitch. Try to avoid stitching into the ribbon.
- Hold the end of the ribbon up and stitch a traveling line beside the secured ribbon to its base.
- At the base, gently hold the end of the ribbon against the needle and jump over it, gathering it. The second ribbon should lay softly against the first ribbon that is laying flat or slightly overlap it.
- Make an additional stitch in place to secure the stitch.
- Stitch a traveling line about ½" in the direction you want the vine to flow.
- Twist ribbon a few times.
- Jump stitch over to secure and take an additional stitch in place to secure the stitch.
- Continue the vines and leaves until you get to the end of the design line.
- Cut ribbons on an angle, thread into chenille needle, pull to back and tie with bobbin threads.

See steps 1 – 4 of Straight Stitch, page 20.
Combination of stem stitches and straight stitches.

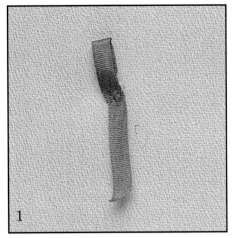

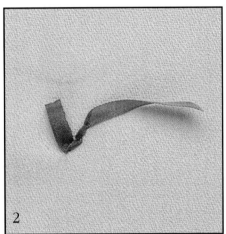

Fern Fronds

The fern frond is several stacked straight stitches on each side of a stem stitched vein. The leaves are usually longer at the base and curve into shorter stitches at the tip. Draw the center line with an even number of leaves on each side. (See Fig. 2, page 14).

Stitch the largest leaf at the base of the fern frond. Continue laying stitches side by side up one edge of the vein to the tip. Turn and repeat the procedure from the smallest leaf at the tip to the largest at the base. To create the vein, twist the ribbon and use the stem stitch back to the tip. Stitch an additional leaf at the center of the tip of the frond.

- Secure ribbon at an angle at the base of the first leaf.
- Lay the ribbon flat and stitch up the center to the tip. Stitch on the ribbon.
- Stitch across the end of the ribbon. Stitch on the ribbon. This is the tip of the leaf.
- Hold the end of ribbon up, travel down the center of the secured ribbon to its base and off to the side.
- Fold the loose end of the ribbon over the top of previously secured ribbon.

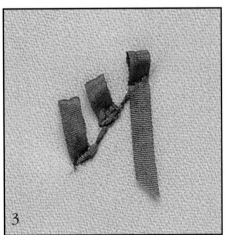

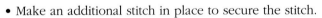

- At the base of the leaf, stitch across the ribbon to secure the top layer of ribbon. Stitch on the ribbon. (#1)
- Twist the ribbon once and lay at an angle away from the previously stitched leaf, toward the next leaf.
- Jump stitch over the twisted ribbon to secure. (#2)

1. Stacked straight stitch.
2. Twist ribbon and jump stitch.
3. Repeat up one side.
4. Complete second side.
5. Stem and vein.
6. Add top leaf.

- Make an additional stitch in place to secure the stitch.
- Extend the ribbon beside the previously stitched leaf and repeat the process. Make each leaf a little smaller than the preceding leaf.
- Continue to the top of one side of the vein. (#3)
- Repeat stitching leaves from the top of the vein to the base on the unstitched side of the fern frond. (#4)
- After securing the last leaf, travel about ½" below the

Silk Ribbons by Machine

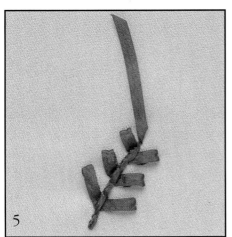 

base of the fern frond to begin the stem.

- Twist the ribbon and secure using a jump stitch.
- Fold the twisted ribbon over itself and back to the base of the fern frond, stacking it as with the leaves.
- Jump stitch to secure. This is the stem.
- Continue the stem stitch up the center of the leaves with a looser twist in the ribbon, making a vein. Lay the ribbon so it covers your previously twisted ribbons. (#5)
- Stitch one additional leaf at the center of the top of the frond. (#6)
- Cut ribbon on an angle, thread into chenille needle, pull to back at the top of the vein, just below the center leaf and tie with bobbin thread. You have completed one fern frond.
- Use the eye end of the chenille needle to separate the top loops from the secured bottom loops.

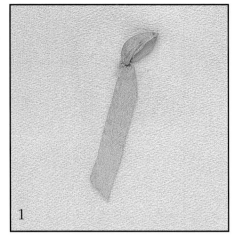

Daisy Flowers

Daisy flowers are created by using the basic straight stitch. Instead of traveling on a vine, just travel from the center out to the tip of a petal, secure with a jump stitch, travel back to the center, and secure with another jump stitch. Slightly rotate the hoop and repeat until the circle is completed and all the petals are stitched.

To make the size daisy you want, draw a circle with your template. There should be five lines from the center of the circle to the outer edge for petals. Daisy flowers usually have an odd number of petals. A "Y" is a good template to use for the stitches. Center a "Y" in the circle. Draw two legs on either side of the "trunk" of the "Y." Stitch to the new five points of the "Y" and return to the center intersection (see Fig. 1, page 14).

1. Straight stitch.
2. Rotate hoop and repeat.
3. Complete motif, add center stitches of choice.

Flat Daisy Flowers

Flat daisy flowers are created the same way as the fern fronds, using the stacked straight stitch. The difference is the ribbons are laid in a circle rather that a curved row and they are all the same length. Use either 4mm or 7mm ribbons. Begin by drawing an outer and inner circle. The center circle will be the base of the petals, while the outer circle will be a guide for the tips of the petals.

- Secure ribbon at the base of the first petal.
- Lay the ribbon flat and stitch up the center of the ribbon to the tip of the petal.
- Stitch across the end of the ribbon. This is the tip of the petal.
- Hold the end of the ribbon up and stitch a traveling line down the center of the secured ribbon to its base.
- Fold the loose end of the ribbon over the top of the previously secured ribbon.
- At the base of the petal, stitch across the ribbon to secure the top ribbon. Secure the stitch.
- Twist ribbon once, jump stitch to secure. Lay the ribbon end at an angle, next to and barely overlapping the base of the previously stitched petal.
- Stitch across the base and repeat the process by rotating the hoop until the circle is completed.
- Cut ribbons on an angle, thread into chenille needle, and pull to back and tie with bobbin threads.
- Fill in center with French knots or bullion stitches.

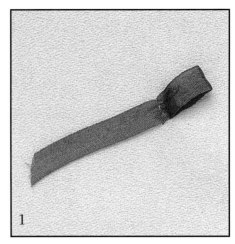

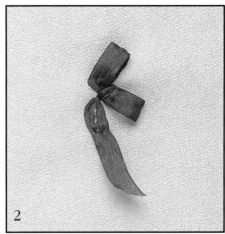

1. Stacked straight stitch.
2. Rotate hoop, twist ribbon, jump stitch at base.
3. Tidy up center, add center stitches of choice.

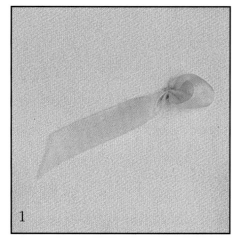

1

2

3

1. Looped straight stitch.
2. Rotate hoop and repeat.
3. Tidy up center, add center stitches of choice.

Looped Daisy Flowers

Looped daisy flowers are created by drawing a circle the approximate size you want the outer edge of the daisy to appear. Draw an inner circle for a base line to secure the ends of the loops. The difference between looped daisy flower and the straight stitch daisy flower is you don't travel to the tips of the petals. If you sometimes forget and travel out to the tip, just travel back to the base and continue. The loops will cover the monofilament thread.

After completing the looped circle, tidy up the center by stitching a tiny circle on top of the ribbons at the base of the loops. If your loops appear longer on one side or you have an oval flower, stitch over the base of the loops to make a neater circle. This will give you a more rounded flower. Also you will have a flatter area to stitch the centers of French knots, bullion knots, or a chain stitched circle.

For a fuller flower, stitch additional loops on top of the previously stitched loops. Fill in sparse areas the same way.

When the flower is full, there is no need for center stitches of French knots. Instead fluff up the loops toward the center.

- Secure the ribbon on the inner circle of the flower. Clip off end.
- Place the ribbon in front of the needle. Jump stitch to the front of the ribbon. Secure the stitch.
- With the tweezers make a loop in the ribbon and place it on the outer circle.
- With the tweezers and the first finger and thumb of your left hand hold the ribbon on its side against the needle.
- Jump stitch across the ribbon and secure the stitch, so the needle is again in front of the ribbon.
- Continue pivoting the hoop, looping, and jump stitching to the front until the flower is completed.
- Secure the last loop, cut the ribbon on an angle, thread into a chenille needle, and pull to back and tie with bobbin thread.

Layered Looped Daisy Flowers

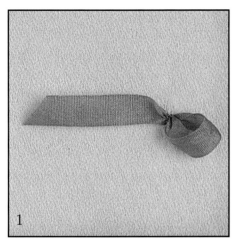

Follow instructions for the looped daisy flowers.

1. Looped straight stitch.

2. Rotate hoop and complete circle.

3. Repeat with second color, no center stitches needed.

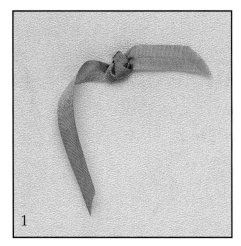

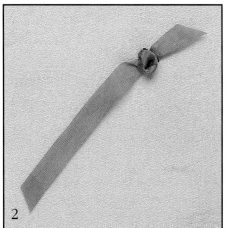

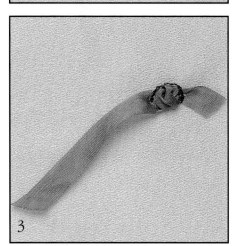

Dainty Tea Roses

The curl and flip stitch will be utilized in creating the rolled and ruffled edges of dainty tea roses. As you relax and allow the ribbons to roll and flow, the roses will appear pretty and natural. Look at photographs of curly tea roses in the seed catalogs to see how they appear. You will be stitching around the rose counter-clockwise; while rotating the hoop clockwise. In each step, rotate the hoop ¼ turn. As the rose becomes larger, make the curls looser. For a fuller rose only stitch about a third of the way across the silk ribbon. This will be approximately three stitches on 7mm and two stitches on 4mm ribbons. Always separate and fluff up the curls after the embroidery is complete.

- Place the needle down in the fabric. Make a few stitches in place to secure the stitch. Tie a loose single knot around the needle 2" from the end with the short end to the right of the needle.
- Place the ends of the ribbon to each side of the needle and hold them down to the throat plate with your fingertips about 1" away from the needle.
- Jump stitch the needle out of the knot. Make a few stitches to secure the stitch.
- With the tweezers, roll the knot so the soft knotted side is up and the tails are flat against the throat plate. (#1)
- Travel around the knot and stitch across the short ribbon end to secure it to the fabric. Trim the end of the ribbon. (#2)
- With the knot on the right side of the needle, travel counterclockwise, stitching close to the knot, until you reach the long end of the ribbon.
- With the tweezers, hold the ribbon so it extends from the bottom side of the knot against the throat plate.
- Stitch toward yourself about halfway across the ribbon then back off the ribbon (where stitching began). (#3)
- Hold the ribbon up toward the knot and slightly angle it toward yourself.
- Stitch under the ribbon, traveling counterclockwise around the knot, rotating the hoop ¼ turn.
- Travel an additional ribbon width close to the knot, rotating the hoop ¼ turn. (#4)
- Allow the ribbon to curl over itself and toward the needle. Softly flip it and hold flat against throat plate with the

1. Tie knot around needle, jump stitch out of knot and roll over.
2. Travel to secure short ribbon end.
3. Travel to secure long ribbon end by stitching on and off.
4. Rotate hoop, travel beside ribbon, plus additional ribbon width.
5. Curl ribbon toward needle. Stitch on and off ribbon.
6. Add more curls.

tweezers (corkscrew effect). The ribbon should appear as it did for your first petal.

- Continue rotating the hoop ¼ turn, curling, flipping, and stitching around the knot until the rose is the size desired. The completed petals will be to the right of the needle. The new stitches will be traveling around the left side of the needle. As the rose gets larger, lay down longer lengths of ribbon, creating fuller petals. (#5)
- To finish, stitch across the ribbon and back as though making a petal, cut ribbon leaving a 3" tail.
- Using the chenille needle, curl the ribbon to the right as though you were making another petal. Pull to the back, leaving a soft roll on the top. Tie with bobbin thread. The tie-off stitch appears as another petal.
- To create the realistic curly tea rose, gently run the tip of one prong of the tweezers inside the curls, slightly separating them. The rose should have slightly separated curly petals, rather than rolls of ribbon around the knot. Fluff up the curls so the background fabric is not showing between the curls.

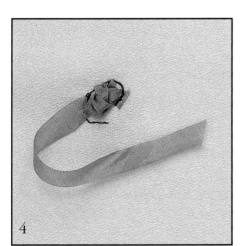

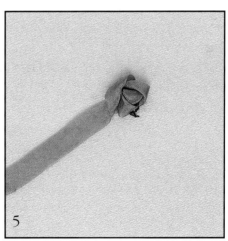

Basic Stitches

Now that you have practiced and accomplished the basic stitches, stitch them using different widths and colors of ribbons. Following are a few examples I challenge you to try.

STRAIGHT STITCH

LEAVES – Hand-dyed ribbons for a realistic effect.

BUDS – 1 stitch of 4mm ribbon for bud with 1 stitch of 7mm green ribbon on each side.

DAISIES – White 4mm or 7mm petals with yellow French knot centers.

SUNFLOWERS – 7mm gold ribbon for petals with dark brown bullion stitch centers.

BLACK EYED SUSAN – 4mm or 7mm gold ribbon for petals with black French knot centers.

PANSIES – 4mm hand-dyed ribbons in purples and yellows with yellow bullion stitch centers.

CLEMATIS – 7mm bright colored ribbons. Large flowers with yellow bullion stitch centers.

STEM STITCH

STEMS – Twist and jump stitch to connect leaves.

VINES – Twist and jump stitch in curves with hand-dyed green ribbons.

CHAIN STITCH

CENTERS – All tiny cords beginning at outer edge and ending in the center.

STAMENS – Tiny cords beginning under a petal and ending with a French knot.

VINES – 2mm, 4mm, and 7mm ribbons. Twist and curve for borders or to connect motifs.

BASKET – All cords depending on the size you want the basket. Variegated 3-ply cords are beautiful. Stitch handle, then the outline of the basket. Continue in a circle, ending in the center.

CURL AND FLIP STITCH

CURLY TEA ROSES – 7mm or 4mm ribbons. Use all colors. Try hand-dyed ribbons for shaded realistic effect.

STATICE – 4mm ribbons. Use all colors. Corkscrew effect on a stem.

HOLLYHOCKS – 7mm and 4mm bright ribbons. Make 7mm corkscrews at bottom and 4mm toward the top.

Mix tiny straight stitch leaves throughout blossoms.

FRENCH KNOT

QUEEN ANNE'S LACE – Ecru or white cords. Make a cluster on top of a stem.

BABY'S BREATH – Tiny ecru or white cords. Make clusters as a fill in where needed. No greenery needed.

CENTERS – All cords, 2mm and 4mm ribbons to fill in the centers of flowers.

PISTILS – Tiny cords at the end of stamens.

GRAPES – Tiny purple variegated cords. Stitch close together in the shape of a free-form triangle.

BULLION STITCH

CENTERS – 4mm ribbons. Allow to coil across ends of each other.

WISTERIA – Hand-dyed ribbons in lavender shades. Lay side by side and allow to overlap in a free-form triangle.

BUDS – 4mm or 7mm ribbon. Make 1 stitch. Add a green straight stitch leaf on each side, overlapping at the base of the bud.

Expanding Basic Stitches

Now the fun begins! You can expand all those glorious stitches to embroider any flowers. Following are a few suggestions to try.

STACKED STRAIGHT STITCH

TULIPS – 4mm or 7mm ribbon. 1 stitch in center, 1 stitch on each side at an outward angle, overlapping at the base.

POINSETTIAS – 7mm ribbon stitch a layer around a circle. 4mm ribbon stitch another layer of shorter stitches on top around the circle. French knots in center.

ZINNIAS – 7mm or 4mm ribbons. Use all colors. French knots in center.

FERNS – 4mm green ribbons.

LOOPED STRAIGHT STITCH

DAHLIAS – 7mm or 4mm ribbons. Mix colors on one flower. French knots in center.

MUMS – 7mm ribbons. Use bright colors. Try hand-dyed ribbons for shaded realistic effect.

MARIGOLDS – 4mm ribbons. Stitch one layer around circle. Change colors and stitch another color on top. Use realistic colored hand-dyed ribbons.

STRAWFLOWERS – 2mm or 4mm ribbons. Make tiny flowers in mixed colors.

BELLFLOWERS – 2mm or 4mm ribbons. Make very full tiny flowers.

CURVED BULLION STITCH

WISTERIA – 7mm or 4mm hand-dyed ribbons in lavender shades. Allow to overlap in a free-form triangle.

GLADIOLUS – 7mm ribbons in bright and pastel shades. Make a stem stitch vine up the center and surround it with an oval of tiny curved bullion stitches. Exaggerate the curves, almost in circles.

HYACINTH – 2mm and 4mm pastel ribbons. Make a stem stitch vine up the center surround it with an oval of very tiny curved bullion stitches. Exaggerate the curved bullion stitches, almost in circles.

QUEEN ANNE'S LACE – 2mm or 4mm ecru or white ribbons. Make a cluster on top of a stem.

Projects

Framed White Daisies

Silk Ribbons by Machine

Framed White Daisies

The framed white daisies motif is embroidered on yellow satin jacquard drapery fabric. It is mounted on a 5" x 7" self-stick mounting foam board, matted with a black mat, and in a wooden frame.

- The vines and leaves are embroidered first so the ends can be covered with petals.
- Leaves are straight stitches with 4mm green ribbon. Stems are stem stitches with the same 4mm green ribbon.
- Daisies are straight stitches with white 4mm ribbon.
- The centers are French knots with a single ply of yellow rayon cord.

Framed Daisy Mixture

Silk Ribbons by Machine

Framed Daisy Mixture

The framed daisy mixture motif is embroidered on ecru antique satin drapery fabric. It is mounted on a 5" x 7" self-stick mounting foam board, matted with a berry colored mat, and in a wooden frame.

- The vines and leaves are embroidered first so the ends can be covered with petals.
- Leaves are straight stitches with 4mm green ribbon. Stems are stem stitches with the same 4mm green ribbon.
- Small daisies are straight stitches with purple and gold 4mm ribbons. The centers are French knots with a single ply of lavender and purple cotton crochet cords.
- Large daisies are straight stitches with lavender, berry, coral, and pink 7mm ribbons. The centers of the lavender daisies are chain stitches with a single ply of pink cotton crochet cord. The centers of the berry daisies are French knots with 4mm of gold ribbon. The centers of the coral and pink daisies are made by cutting the end of the ribbon, leaving a 3" tail. Take the end of the ribbon across the center of the daisies and to the back with the chenille needle, then secure with bobbin thread. Fluff up the stitch with the eye end of the chenille needle.
- The baby's breath is a cluster of French knots with a single ply of blue variegated cotton crochet cord.

Corduroy Wisteria Vest

Corduroy Wisteria Vest

The wisteria clusters are embroidered on a purchased deep burgundy wide wale corduroy vest. The vine flows from one shoulder to the center front, just below the dart. It picks up again in the center of the opposite side and flows below the dart toward the side. Even though there is a front opening, the flowers have continuity because of the positioning of the vines. Wine thread is used in the bobbin and blends in very well with the lining.

- The leaves and vines are stitched first, then a curved vine of very loose stem stitches down the wisteria cluster.
- Leaves are straight stitches with 7mm hand-dyed green ribbon. Stems are stem stitches with the same 7mm hand-dyed green ribbon.

- The wisteria clusters are curved bullion stitches with 7mm hand-dyed lavender ribbon. Just before the motif is completed, integrate a 4mm lilac ribbon into the cluster to add light tones.

Yellow Daisy Pillow

Yellow Daisy Pillow

The motif is embroidered on an 8" square Battenberg lace doily. It is machine stitched along the edge of the cotton fabric center to a square of yellow satin jacquard drapery fabric, leaving the lace edging loose and free. Before constructing the 12" pillow, a white rayon braid was inserted in the seam.

- The vines and leaves are embroidered first so the ends can be covered with petals.
- Leaves are straight stitches with 2mm green ribbon. Stems are stem stitches with the same 2mm green ribbon.
- Small daisies are straight stitches with berry, gold, light blue, dark blue, and yellow hand-dyed 4mm ribbons. The centers are French knots with a single ply of yellow, berry, gold, and white rayon cords.
- Large daisies are straight stitches with 7mm yellow, orange hand-dyed, and yellow hand-dyed ribbons. The center of the yellow daisy is curved bullion stitches with 4mm dark blue ribbon. The centers of the orange hand-dyed daisies are chain stitches with a single ply of yellow rayon cord. The center of the yellow hand-dyed daisy is curved bullion stitches with 4mm orange ribbon.
- The three petal daisy is straight stitches with 7mm berry ribbon.
- The baby's breath is a cluster of French knots with a single ply of blue variegated cotton crochet cord.

Green Daisy Pillow

Silk Ribbons by Machine

Green Daisy Pillow

The green daisy pillow motif is embroidered on a 10" oval Battenberg lace doily. It is machine stitched along the edge of the cotton fabric center to a square of green satin jacquard drapery fabric, leaving the lace edging loose and free. A 12" square pillow was then constructed.

- The vines and leaves are embroidered first so the ends can be covered with petals.
- Leaves are straight stitches with 7mm green ribbon. Stems are stem stitches with the same 7mm green ribbon.
- Three small daisies are straight stitches with fuschia, yellow, and dark blue 4mm ribbons. The centers are French knots with a single ply of white, lavender, and white rayon cords.
- One small daisy is looped straight stitches with white 4mm ribbon. The center is French knots with a single ply of blue variegated cotton crochet cord.
- Five large daisies are straight stitches with peach, red, lavender, light blue, and purple 7mm ribbons. The centers are French knots with a single ply of aqua, black, navy blue, red, and yellow rayon cords.
- Two large daisies are looped straight stitches with gold and blue 4mm ribbons. The centers are French knots with brown and purple 2-ply cotton cords.

Silk Ribbons by Machine

Lavender Battenberg Lace Pillow

Lavender Battenberg Lace Pillow

This flower motif is embroidered on a 10" oval Battenberg lace doily, which is centered on a hand-dyed 16" Battenberg lace doily. A thin layer of batting was placed behind the cotton center embroidered area to prevent the lavender lace from showing. The embroidered doily is machine stitched along the edge of the cotton fabric center, leaving the lace edging loose and free. The large lavender Battenberg lace doily is straight stitched with matching thread to the top of a white 14" cotton pillow, leaving the outer lace edges free.

- The vines and leaves are embroidered first so the ends can be covered with petals.
- Leaves are straight stitches with 7mm pastel green ribbon. Stems are stem stitches with the same 7mm pastel green ribbon.
- The small daisies are straight stitches with yellow and lavender 4mm ribbons. The centers are French knots with a single ply of blue and white rayon cords.
- Three large daisies are straight stitches with lavender, pink, and light blue 7mm ribbons.

The centers are French knots with yellow, wine, and navy blue 2-ply cotton cords.
- One large daisy is looped straight stitches with blue 4mm ribbon. The center is French knots with a single ply of white rayon cord. One large daisy is layered looped straight stitches with yellow 4mm ribbon, then white 4mm ribbon. The center is French knots with wine 2-ply cotton cord.
- The three petal daisy is straight stitches with 7mm wine ribbon.

Silk Ribbons by Machine

White Battenberg Lace Pillow

White Battenberg Lace Pillow

This is an excellent first project for a sampler using all the basic stitches illustrated in the book. Tiny motifs are centered on doilies then arranged on a pillow top.

- The center motif of the white Battenberg lace pillow is embroidered on an 8" round Battenberg lace doily, which is centered on a 16" Battenberg lace doily. Four 4" Battenberg lace doilies with silk ribbon embroidered centers are stitched in each corner of the large doily. To give dimension, a thin layer of batting was placed behind the cotton embroidered area of the center doily. Each silk ribbon embroidered doily is machine stitched along the edge of the cotton fabric center, leaving the lace edging loose and free. The large Battenberg lace doily is straight stitched to the top of a white 14" cotton pillow, leaving the outer lace edges free.

- The center doily consists of straight stitches, stem stitches, and French knots.

- The vines and leaves are embroidered first so the ends can be covered with petals. Leaves are straight stitches with 7mm green ribbon. Stems are stem stitches with the same 7mm green ribbon. The daisies are straight stitches with yellow hand-dyed 4mm ribbon. The centers are French knots with brown 2-ply cotton cord.

- DOILY # 1 – consists of straight stitches, stem stitches, curl and flip stitches, and French knots.

- DOILY #2 – consists of straight stitches, stem stitches, looped straight stitches, and French knots.

- DOILY # 3 – consists of straight stitches, stem stitches, and curved bullion stitches.

- DOILY #4 – consists of stacked straight stitches, stacked fern stitches, and curved bullion stitches.

DOILY #1

DOILY #2

CENTER DOILY

DOILY #3

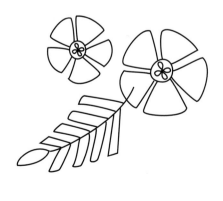

DOILY #4

Woven Basket of Blossoms

Woven Basket of Blossoms

The woven basket of blossoms motif is embroidered on a 14" round Battenberg lace doily. It is machine stitched along the edge of the cotton fabric center to a square of wine velvet fabric, leaving the lace edging loose and free. A 16" square pillow is then constructed.

Basket

The basket is created by stitching a continuous chain stitch with three plys of wine variegated cotton cord. The handle is stitched first, then the outer edge of the basket. Fill in the center by continuing the chain stitch in a circle from the outer edge toward the center. Allow the rows of stitches to butt up against each other but not overlap.

Fill with Flowers

- The vines and leaves are embroidered first so the ends can be covered with petals.
- Large leaves are straight stitches with 7mm pastel green ribbon. Stems are stem stitches with the same 7mm pastel green ribbon. Small leaves are straight stitches with three different 4mm green ribbons. Stems are stem stitches with the same 4mm green ribbons used for the small leaves.
- The large dainty tea rose is curl and flip stitches with 7mm red ribbon. The medium dainty tea rose is curl and flip stitches with 7mm pink ribbon.
- The tulips are three straight stitches with 7mm yellow and blue ribbons. On the yellow tulip, the stamens are chain stitches and the pistils are French knots with a single ply of black rayon cord.
- One daisy is straight stitches with 7mm lavender ribbon. The center is chain stitches with a single ply of white rayon cord.
- One daisy is straight stitches with 7mm hand-dyed purple ribbon. The center is

French knots with a single ply of yellow rayon cord.
- The frilly mum is looped straight stitches with dark blue 4mm ribbon. There is no center, just fluffed ribbons.
- The cluster flower hanging over the edge of the basket is curved bullion stitches with lavender and yellow hand-dyed ribbon.
- The baby's breath across the top of the handle of the basket is French knots with variegated 2-ply cotton cord. The stems are chain stitches with a single ply of green cotton cord.

Silk Ribbons by Machine

White Battenberg Lace Vest

White Battenberg Lace Vest

The silk ribbon is embroidered on a purchased Battenberg lace vest. Before embroidering, a piece of muslin was stitched along the outside edges to allow more room for hooping. The plastic buttons are replaced with buttons from a trinket stash.

- The vines and leaves are embroidered first so the ends can be covered with petals.
- Leaves are straight stitches with 7mm bright green ribbon. Stems are stem stitches with the same 7mm bright green ribbon.
- Two large daisies are straight stitches with 7mm blue and red ribbons. The center of the blue daisy is chain stitches with a single ply of white rayon cord. The center of the red daisy is French knots with a single ply of yellow rayon cord.
- One medium daisy is one layer of straight stitches with 4mm dark yellow ribbon; then another layer of straight stitches with 4mm light yellow ribbon, alternating petal colors. The center is curved bullion stitches with 4mm dark blue ribbon.
- One medium daisy is stacked straight stitches with 7mm pink ribbon. The center is French knots with 2-ply purple cotton cord.
- One tiny daisy is straight stitches with 4mm dark blue ribbon. The center is French knots with a single ply of red rayon cord.
- The three frilly mums are layered looped straight stitches. They are dark and light orange, dark and light purple, and dark and light blue 4mm ribbons. There are no center stitches only fluffed ribbon.

Porcelain Doll Dress

Silk Ribbons by Machine

Porcelain Doll Dress

The 18" porcelain doll is made from a kit. The dress is a modified version of the pattern in the kit. It is constructed of dusty blue satin moiré with lace and pearl trim. The center area separated by lace is the portion embellished with the silk ribbon embroidery.

- The vines and leaves are embroidered first so the ends can be covered with petals.
- Leaves are straight stitches with 4mm green ribbon. Stems are stem stitches with the same 4mm green ribbon.
- The dainty tea roses are all embroidered with 4mm silk ribbons. The different sizes are created by the number of curls stitched around the knot.

Project Ideas

May I suggest a few ways to utilize your new skill now that you have relaxed and mastered the wonderful silk ribbon stitches in this book.

ON READY MADES

Purchase ready mades and embroider silk ribbon motifs on collars, cuffs, pockets, and yokes. Use matching thread in the bobbin so they will have a finished appearance of which you can be proud.

ON LACE

Besides Battenberg doilies with the unembroidered areas in the centers, look for other types of doilies and laces to embellish with silk ribbon flowers. Crocheted doilies with large holes can be embellished with silk ribbons by first stitching the doily to a background fabric, then hooping and embroidering. This way the stitches won't get lost in the holes.

Machine stitch the finished doilies to a craft project or to ready mades. Hand stitch if you want to place it in an area which is hard to maneuver with the machine.

The finished doilies are also beautiful on craft boxes. After finishing the silk ribbon embroidery, stitch a thin layer of batting behind the center area. Glue the batted area to the top of a decorated box or jewelry box, leaving the lace edges free and loose. Embellish with purchased braids, ribbons, and trinkets.

Tiny doilies create wonderful Christmas ornaments by lining the back and adding a ribbon hanger.

ON RIBBONS

The silk ribbon motifs are elegant when embroidered on wide satin and grosgrain ribbons, then used to embellish clothing and home decor. This technique will embellish anything which cannot be hooped. Try the wide ribbons on hats, purses, belts, and clothing. Make the ribbon large enough to fit into the hoop with the muslin strips, then remove them when the embroidery is finished. Attach the ribbons by straight stitching, using built in machine embroidery stitches, or gluing them to craft items.

ADD TO MACHINE STITCHES

The majority of the sewing machines today have some automatic embroidery stitches. Embellish these with the use of silk ribbon embroidery. Allow the machine to do the leaves and vines, then layer beautiful dimensional silk flowers on top. Create connecting vines with the machine stitches and randomly place silk ribbons on them. Embellishing in this way will add your personal touch.

VINTAGE LACES AND LINENS

Go to the attic and retrieve some old linens, even the damaged ones. Embellish the centers of crocheted dresser scarves with silk ribbons. Cut out the good parts of old ragged doilies, embroider silk ribbons on them and use to embellish clothing and crazy quilts. If you don't want to cut them, stitch them down to a background and embroider flowers on the damaged areas.

IRON-ON TRANSFERS

Craft stores carry Victorian iron-on transfers for cloth. I think the transfers are pretty but are lacking something. A wonderful way to embellish them is to use the silk ribbon flowers as a border. For an elegant home decor item, apply the transfer according to the package instructions to a Victorian fabric such as satin moiré. A curved 7mm ribbon chain stitch embellishes nicely with flowers scattered randomly on it. Frame the motif in a Victorian-style frame.

There is no end to what you can create once you get started thinking and looking around for something to embellish.

Have a wonderful time creating you own "Romantic Ribbons."

Heart-shaped Velveteen Pincushion

This section includes photos of projects with suggestions to inspire your creativity. Use the photographs for ideas and positioning of your own designs. Each project has a general description. You can use the size ribbons and colors of your choice. Sketch your own patterns or use the ones from the detailed projects.

The heart-shaped velveteen pincushion motif is embroidered on a 7" gold velveteen heart-shaped pillow. After the silk ribbon embroidery was completed and the pillow was constructed, a dark green satin braid was hand stitched along the seam line.

• The vines and leaves are embroidered first

so the ends can be covered with petals.

• Leaves are straight stitches with 2mm green ribbon. Stems are stem stitches with the same 2mm green ribbon.

• The large roses are curl and flip stitches with 7mm pink and lavender ribbons. The medium roses are curl and flip stitches with wine, berry, and dark blue 4mm ribbons. The tiny roses are curl and flip stitches with 4mm light blue ribbon. The Queen Anne's lace is curved bullion stitches with 4mm white ribbon.

Heart-shaped Dainty Tea Rose Pillow

The dainty tea rose motif is embroidered on an 11" heart-shaped crocheted doily. To prevent losing the ribbon flowers in the holes, the doily is machine stitched, just inside the scalloped edge, to green satin jacquard drapery fabric, leaving the lace edging loose and free. Both layers are hooped and embroidered. A heart-shaped pillow is then constructed.

- The vines and leaves are embroidered first so the ends can be covered with petals.
- Leaves are straight stitches with 7mm ribbon the same color green as the background fabric. Stems are stem stitches with the same 7mm green ribbon.
- The dainty tea roses are curl and flip stitches with 7mm red, coral, and peach ribbons.

The sizes are varied by the number of curls stitched. The largest red tea roses have very loose stitches toward the outside rows of curls. They are 1½" across.

Daisy Denim Vest

The mixture of daisies is embroidered on a purchased light blue denim vest. Before embroidering, a piece of muslin is stitched along the outside edges to allow more room for hooping.

- The vines and leaves are embroidered first so the ends can be covered with petals.
- Leaves are straight stitches with 7mm bright green ribbon. Stems are stem stitches with the same 7mm bright green ribbon.
- The daisies are a variety of all the daisy stitches. The largest mum is layered looped straight stitches with hand-dyed purple and yellow ribbon.
- Charms were added by hand in complimentary areas within the flowers. Stitching with metallic thread the color of the charms gives a very professional touch to the embellishment. Thread about 20" of thread in a hand needle and double and knot. While pulling the stitches, grasp the thread, rather than the needle. If there is too much stress on the fine thread, the needle eye can cut it. Tie both ends of the threads together to prevent them from coming unstitched, then clip ends.

"Everyone Loves a Barn Raising" Mini-Log Cabin Quilt

The 17" square mini-quilt consists of 36 – 2" Log Cabin blocks arranged in the Barn Raising pattern. It is pieced with with cream and black print and solid black cotton fabrics. It is bordered with identical red and black print and solid black cotton fabrics. Red and black print hearts are hand appliquéd in the corners.

- Dainty tea roses are embroidered on rambling vines across the Log Cabin blocks. The leaves and vines are straight stitches with 7mm hand-dyed green ribbon. The dainty tea roses are curl and flip stitches with 7mm hand-dyed purple, gold, and cream ribbons. The size variations are determined by the

number of curls and the looseness of the stitches.

- A rambling vine along the border is chain stitches with three plys of green variegated cotton cord.

Credits / Suppliers

English Sewing Machine Company

7001 Benton Road

Paducah, KY 42003

(502) 898-7301

Web of Thread

1410 Broadway

Paducah, KY 42001

(502) 575-9700

Pfaff American Sales Corporation

610 Winters Avenue

Paramus, NJ 07653

Sulky of America

3113D Broadpoint Drive

Harbor Heights, FL 33983

AQS Books on Quilts

This is only a partial listing of the books on quilts that are available from the American Quilter's Society. AQS books are known the world over for their timely topics, clear writing, beautiful color photographs, and accurate illustrations and patterns. Most of the following books are available from your local bookseller, quilt shop, or public library. If you are unable to locate certain titles in your area, you may order by mail from the AMERICAN QUILTER'S SOCIETY, P.O. Box 3290, Paducah, KY 42002-3290. Customers with Visa or MasterCard may phone in orders from 7:00–4:00 CST, Monday–Friday, Toll Free 1-800-626-5420. Add $2.00 for postage for the first book ordered and $0.40 for each additional book. Include item number, title, and price when ordering. Allow 14 to 21 days for delivery.

2282	**Adapting Architectural Details for Quilts,** Carol Wagner	$12.95
1907	**American Beauties: Rose & Tulip Quilts,** Marston & Cunningham	$14.95
4543	**American Quilt Blocks: 50 Patterns for 50 States,** Beth Summers	$18.95
4696	**Amish Kinder Komforts** Betty Havig	$14.95
2121	**Appliqué Designs: My Mother Taught Me to Sew,** Faye Anderson	$12.95
3790	**Appliqué Patterns from Native American Beadwork Designs,** Dr. Joyce Mori	$14.95
2122	**The Art of Hand Appliqué,** Laura Lee Fritz	$14.95
2099	**Ask Helen: More About Quilting Designs,** Helen Squire	$14.95
2207	**Award-Winning Quilts: 1985-1987**	$24.95
2354	**Award-Winning Quilts: 1988-1989**	$24.95
3425	**Award-Winning Quilts: 1990-1991**	$24.95
3791	**Award-Winning Quilts: 1992-1993**	$24.95
4593	**Blossoms by the Sea: Making Ribbon Flowers for Quilts,** Faye Labanaris	$24.95
4697	**Caryl Bryer Fallert: A Spectrum of Quilts, 1983-1995,** Caryl Bryer Fallert	$24.95
3926	**Celtic Style Floral Appliqué** Scarlett Rose	$14.95
2208	**Classic Basket Quilts,** Elizabeth Porter & Marianne Fons	$16.95
2355	**Creative Machine Art,** Sharee Dawn Roberts	$24.95
1820	**Dear Helen, Can You Tell Me?...** Helen Squire	$12.95
3870	**Double Wedding Ring Quilts: New Quilts from an Old Favorite**	$14.95
3399	**Dye Painting!** Ann Johnston	$19.95
2030	**Dyeing & Overdyeing of Cotton Fabrics,** Judy Mercer Tescher	$9.95
3468	**Encyclopedia of Pieced Quilt Patterns,** compiled by Barbara Brackman	$34.95
3846	**Fabric Postcards** Judi Warren	$22.95
4594	**Firm Foundations: Techniques & Quilt Blocks for Precision Piecing,** Jane Hall & Dixie Haywood	$18.95
2356	**Flavor Quilts for Kids to Make** Jennifer Amor	$12.95
2381	**From Basics to Binding: A Complete Guide to Making Quilts,** Karen Kay Buckley	$16.95
4526	**Gatherings: America's Quilt Heritage,** Kathlyn F. Sullivan	$34.95
2097	**Heirloom Miniatures,** Tina M. Gravatt	$9.95
4628	**Helen's Guide to quilting in the 21st century,** Helen Squire	$16.95
2120	**The Ins and Outs: Perfecting the Quilting Stitch,** Patricia J. Morris	$9.95
1906	**Irish Chain Quilts: A Workbook of Irish Chains** Joyce B. Peaden	$14.95
3784	**Jacobean Appliqué: Book I, "Exotica,"** Patricia B. Campbell & Mimi Ayars, Ph.D	$18.95
4544	**Jacobean Appliqué: Book II, "Romantica,"** Patricia B. Campbell & Mimi Ayars, Ph.D	$18.95
3904	**The Judge's Task: How Award-Winning Quilts Are Selected,** Patricia J. Morris	$19.95
4523	**Log Cabin Quilts: New Quilts from an Old Favorite**	$14.95
4545	**Log Cabin with a Twist,** Barbara T. Kaempfer	$18.95
4598	**Love to Quilt: Men's Vests,** Alexandra Capadalis Dupré	$14.95
4753	**Love to Quilt: Historical Penny Squares,** Willa Baranowski	$12.95
2206	**Marbling Fabrics for Quilts** Kathy Fawcett & Carol Shoaf	$12.95
4514	**Mola Techniques for Today's Quilters,** Charlotte Patera	$18.95
3330	**More Projects and Patterns: A Second Collection of Favorite Quilts,** Judy Florence	$18.95
1981	**Nancy Crow: Quilts and Influences,** Nancy Crow	$29.95
3331	**Nancy Crow: Work in Transition,** Nancy Crow	$12.95
3332	**New Jersey Quilts – 1777 to 1950: Contributions to an American Tradition,** The Heritage Quilt Project of New Jersey	$29.95
3927	**New Patterns from Old Architecture,** Carol Wagner	$12.95
2153	**No Dragons on My Quilt,** Jean Ray Laury	$12.95
4598	**Ohio Star Quilts: New Quilts from an Old Favorite**	$16.95
3469	**Old Favorites in Miniature,** Tina Gravatt	$15.95
4515	**Paint and Patches: Painting on Fabrics with Pigment,** Vicki L. Johnson	$18.95
3333	**A Patchwork of Pieces: An Anthology of Early Quilt Stories 1845-1940,** complied by Cuesta Ray Benberry and Carol Pinney Crabb	$14.95
4513	**Plaited Patchwork,** Shari Cole	$19.95
3928	**Precision Patchwork for Scrap Quilts,** Jeannette Tousley Muir	$12.95
4779	**Protecting Your Quilts: A Guide for Quilt Owners, Second Edition**	$6.95
4542	**A Quilted Christmas,** edited by Bonnie Browning	$18.95
2380	**Quilter's Registry,** Lynne Fritz	$9.95
3467	**Quilting Patterns from Native American Designs,** Dr. Joyce Mori	$12.95
3470	**Quilting with Style: Principles for Great Pattern Design,** Marston & Cunningham	$24.95
2284	**Quiltmaker's Guide: Basics & Beyond,** Carol Doak	$19.95
2257	**Quilts: The Permanent Collection – MAQS**	$9.95
3793	**Quilts: The Permanent Collection – MAQS, Volume II**	$9.95
3789	**Roots, Feathers & Blooms: 4-Block Quilts, Their History & Patterns, Book I,** Linda Carlson	$16.95
4512	**Sampler Quilt Blocks from Native American Designs,** Dr. Joyce Mori	$14.95
3796	**Seasons of the Heart & Home: Quilts for a Winter's Day,** Jan Patek	$18.95
3761	**Seasons of the Heart & Home: Quilts for Summer Days,** Jan Patek	$18.95
2357	**Sensational Scrap Quilts,** Darra Duffy Williamson	$24.95
3375	**Show Me Helen...How to Use Quilting Designs,** Helen Squire	$15.95
1790	**Somewhere in Between: Quilts and Quilters of Illinois,** Rita Barrow Barber	$14.95
3794	**Spike & Zola: Patterns Designed for Laughter...and Appliqué, Painting, or Stenciling,** Donna French Collins	$9.95
3929	**The Stori Book of Embellishing,** Mary Stori	$16.95
3903	**Straight Stitch Machine Appliqué,** Letty Martin	$16.95
3792	**Striplate Piecing: Piecing Circle Designs with Speed and Accuracy,** Debra Wagner	$24.95
3930	**Tessellations & Variations: Creating One-Patch and Two-Patch Quilts,** Barbara Ann Caron	$14.95
3788	**Three-Dimensional Appliqué and Embroidery Embellishment: Techniques for Today's Album Quilt,** Anita Shackelford	$24.95
4596	**Ties, Ties, Ties: Traditional Quilts from Neckties,** Janet B. Elwin	$19.95
3931	**Time-Span Quilts: New Quilts from Old Tops,** Becky Herdle	$16.95
2029	**A Treasury of Quilting Designs,** Linda Goodmon Emery	$14.95
3847	**Tricks with Chintz: Using Large Prints to Add New Magic to Traditional Quilt Blocks,** Nancy S. Breland	$14.95
2286	**Wonderful Wearables: A Celebration of Creative Clothing,** Virginia Avery	$24.95